EMERGENCY WORKERS

EMT

by
Jim Ollhoff

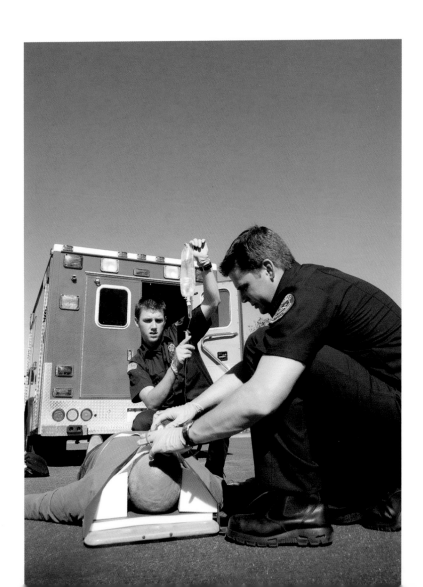

VISIT US AT:
WWW.ABDOPUBLISHING.COM

Printed in the United States of America, North Mankato, Minnesota.
042012
092012

 PRINTED ON RECYCLED PAPER

Editor: John Hamilton
Graphic Design: Sue Hamilton
Cover Design: Neil Klinepier
Cover Photo: iStockPhoto
Interior Photos and Illustrations: AP-pgs 11, 17, 18-19, 24, 26 & 27; Corbis-pgs 15
& 23; Getty-pg 22; Glow Images-pgs 1, 6, 12, 14, 16, 22, 25 & 29; Houston Police
Museum-pg 10 (top); iStockphoto-pgs 16, 20, 21 & 24; Library of Congress-pg 8,
National Academy of Sciences-pg 10 (bottom); Thinkstock-pgs 3, 4, 5, 6, 7, 8, 13, 20, 28
& 32, U.S. Army-pg 27.

ABDO Booklinks

To learn more about Emergency Workers, visit ABDO Publishing Company online. Web
sites about Emergency Workers are featured on our Book Links pages. These links are
routinely monitored and updated to provide the most current information available.
Web site: www.abdopublishing.com

Library of Congress Cataloging-in-Publication Data

Ollhoff, Jim, 1959-
   EMT / Jim Ollhoff.
      p. cm. -- (Emergency workers)
   Includes index.
   ISBN 978-1-61783-512-4
   1. Emergency medical technicians--Juvenile literature. 2. Emergency medicine--Juvenile
literature. I. Title.
   RC86.5.O45 2013
   616.02'5--dc23
                        2012005327

TABLE OF CONTENTS

THE EMT

Adriver is talking on his cell phone on a busy highway. Without realizing it, his car drifts across the lane and bumps into another car. That car careens into oncoming traffic, crashing into two other cars. Other fast-moving cars screech on their brakes, causing more accidents, crashes, and injuries. It's a multi-car pile-up, with many injuries. What happens next?

People call 911 and run to the scene, but they know they shouldn't move anyone. Soon, sirens are heard 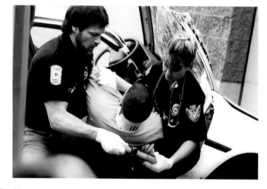 in the distance. Police are the first on the scene to assess the damage and injuries. But the police know they have to clear a path for the Emergency Medical Technicians (EMTs).

The EMTs arrive on the scene and immediately go to work. They quickly determine who is hurt worst, and who needs medical help right away. The EMTs help the injured and get them ready to go to the hospital.

As first responders, EMTs are always ready to help.

WHAT DOES AN EMT DO?

EMTs stabilize an accident victim's head with a neck brace before they attempt to move her.

Emergency Medical Technicians are the first medical people on the scene of an accident or disaster. They are trained in emergency medicine, and know how to treat people in crisis situations. Giving people quick medical help increases their chances of recovery. The EMTs get people stable, and then transport them to a hospital, where doctors and nurses take over.

EMTs might be employed by a local fire department, a hospital, a private ambulance service, or other organization. Some EMTs are volunteers. Others do the job as a paid career. Their exact job duties vary from state to state, and their training might have slight differences, but they all have very important responsibilities.

Depending on the situation, EMTs may have to work to control the bleeding of an injured person. If a person has a heart attack, EMTs may have to monitor their heart rhythm and other vital signs. They may have to try to revive someone who has drowned. They may have to splint a broken bone so that it isn't damaged further on the ride to the hospital.

Fire department EMTs secure a patient for transport in an ambulance.

HISTORY OF EMERGENCY MEDICINE

Ambulances were first used in the mid-1800s. Their only task was to transport injured people to a hospital. The idea of giving emergency medical care on the scene was still unknown. If someone was injured, the first care they received was in the hospital. That idea continued until the mid-1900s.

In wartime, the medical personnel knew that when a wounded soldier received fast

A horse-drawn ambulance used by the U.S. Army in 1908.

medical attention, his chances of survival improved. However, that idea took a long time to make it to the city streets of North America.

In the years before 1966, the field of emergency medicine was not yet born. Some areas of North America had no ambulance service or emergency medicine. In areas that had ambulances, the drivers often had no medical training. In fact, in many cases local funeral directors were also ambulance drivers, since they were the only ones with cars big enough to have someone lie down inside.

A 1958 Cadillac used as both an ambulance and a hearse.

Texas's Houston Police Department dispatch center takes calls in the 1950s. In the past, most medical emergency calls came through police or fire departments. The 911 emergency number started in 1968. Today, nearly all Americans have access to 911.

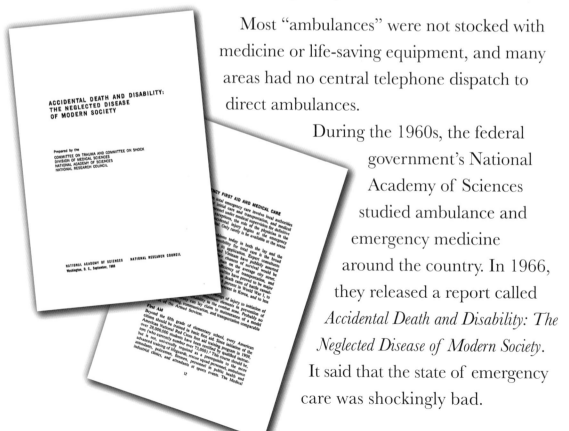

Most "ambulances" were not stocked with medicine or life-saving equipment, and many areas had no central telephone dispatch to direct ambulances.

During the 1960s, the federal government's National Academy of Sciences studied ambulance and emergency medicine around the country. In 1966, they released a report called *Accidental Death and Disability: The Neglected Disease of Modern Society.* It said that the state of emergency care was shockingly bad.

The country was fighting the Vietnam War at the time, and the report made several comparisons to the war. The report said it was better to be wounded on the battlefield in Vietnam than to be in a car accident on America's streets!

The report made a lot of recommendations. Emergency care needed to begin on the scene by medically trained individuals. Ambulances were constructed and stocked, and EMT training began across the country. As a result of that report, the field of Emergency Medical Services (EMS) was born.

A man is treated by a Los Angeles, California, ambulance worker in 1964. Few United States cities had emergency care available to their citizens at that time.

DIFFERENT KINDS OF EMTs

The types and training of EMTs varies from state to state. However, there are usually three kinds of EMTs: basic, intermediate, and paramedic.

EMT-Basic is the first level of training. It usually requires about 50 to 100 hours of classroom instruction, with a written exam and a skills exam. EMTs with this level of training are taught how to control bleeding. They can give extra oxygen to victims when needed. They know how to put on a temporary splint if a bone is broken. When people have back or neck injuries, further movement can permanently damage them. So, EMTs are trained how to immobilize a patient's neck and get them on a backboard and stretcher so they can be transported to the hospital. Basic EMTs are trained in first aid. They can give emergency care if someone has a heart attack or stroke. Sometimes, Basic EMTs can give drugs when there is a life-threatening situation, when seconds count, such as during severe allergic reactions.

Basic EMT training teaches responders how to administer first aid, such as controlling bleeding.

EMT-Intermediate is the next level of training. The classroom hours vary from state to state, but usually require 350 classroom hours or more. The Intermediate EMT has all the training of the EMT-Basic, and more. The Intermediate EMT can give more medications. If a person is unconscious but not breathing, the Intermediate EMT may be able to insert a tube down the person's throat to help them breathe. The Intermediate EMT does more monitoring of a patient's heart, and so can help people who have heart attacks. They can also help women who are giving birth before they can get to a hospital.

Intermediate EMTs are trained to help unconscious victims who are not breathing.

The EMT-Paramedic is the highest level of emergency medical training. These EMTs study for up to two years, often as part of a college degree. They have all the training of a Basic and Intermediate EMT, plus much more. They have additional training in human anatomy. They can give many more

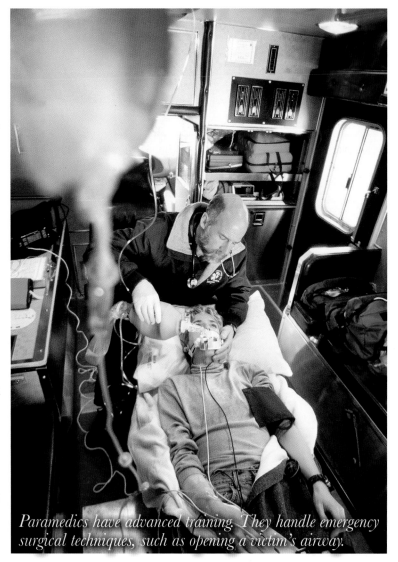

Paramedics have advanced training. They handle emergency surgical techniques, such as opening a victim's airway.

medications. In some areas, they can even prescribe a limited number of drugs. They can perform emergency surgical techniques, such as opening up an airway if a person's throat has closed.

EMTs work closely with doctors, especially doctors who have been trained in emergency medicine. EMTs want to transport injured and sick people to a hospital as soon as possible. However, when an injured or sick person is badly hurt or might die before they get to the hospital, then a well-trained EMT is the best person for the job.

TRAINING

Most EMT training programs require graduation from high school. EMT study programs can be taught during the day, or on evenings and weekends. Classes are often taught in community centers and colleges.

Training teaches EMTs what to do when they arrive at an accident scene. Injured people are often unable to talk. They can't tell an EMT what's wrong. The EMT has to watch for clues, such as the look and feel of a person's skin, or the way they are breathing. The EMT might have to open up the person's eyelid and examine the size of their pupils, which can give clues to their condition.

An EMT must first check if an injured person is breathing, and if their heart is beating. If an injured person is bleeding, the EMT must immediately work to control blood loss.

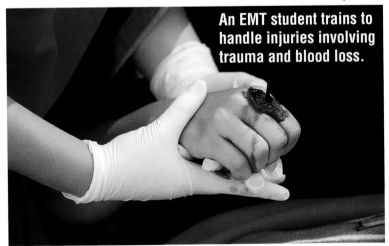

An EMT student trains to handle injuries involving trauma and blood loss.

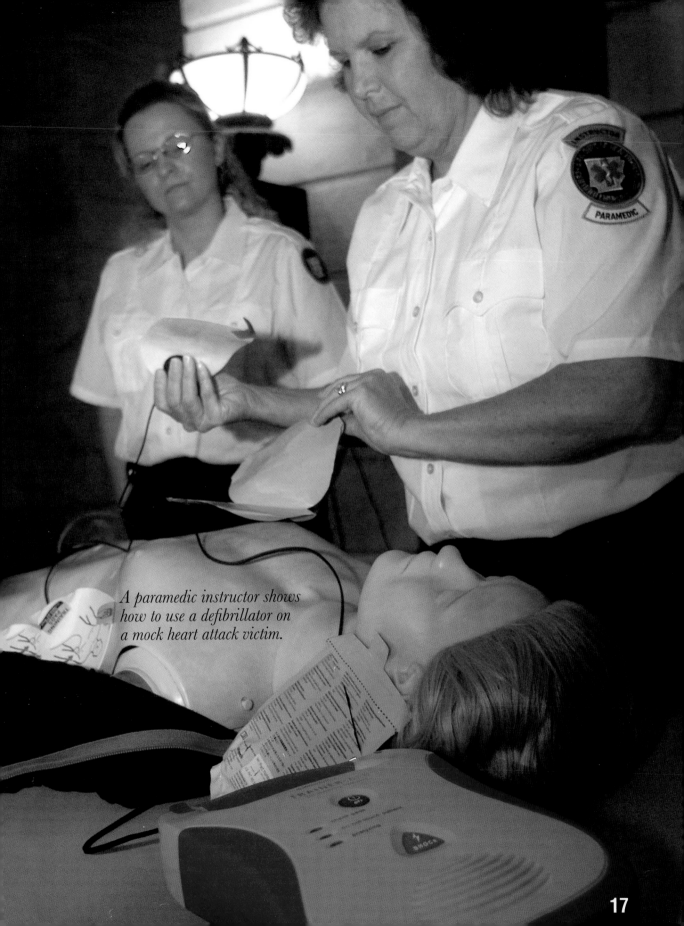

A paramedic instructor shows how to use a defibrillator on a mock heart attack victim.

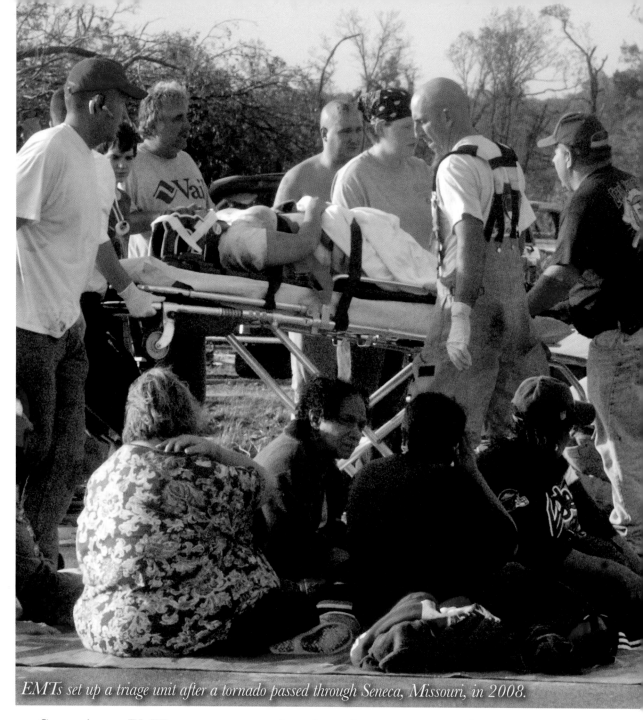

EMTs set up a triage unit after a tornado passed through Seneca, Missouri, in 2008.

Sometimes, EMTs come upon a situation where many people are hurt at the same time. Perhaps there was a multiple car crash, or there was an explosion, or a building collapsed in an earthquake. When many people are involved, all with different kinds of injuries, then the EMT has to do *triage*.

Triage means that EMTs need to make some quick decisions about priorities. Who is hurt worst? Who has non-life-threatening injuries? Who is hurt so severely that they need immediate medical help, and who can wait?

Training is very important, and the knowledge that EMTs have can save many lives. However, some things can't be taught in the classroom. EMTs need to keep calm in emergency situations. They need to complete their duties and communicate clearly while staying calm. EMTs can't panic even if people around them are panicking.

EMT training varies from state to state, and region to region. Most states require that EMTs continue to get more training every year to keep up their certification. States today are working toward a national system of training and certification, so that EMTs across the country will have similar knowledge and duties.

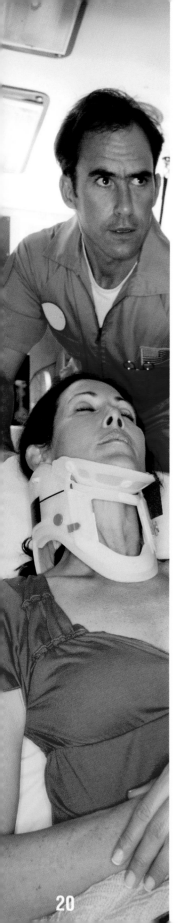

THE MANY JOBS OF AN EMT

Emergency Medical Technicians have many career paths. Some work for fire departments, others for ambulance services or hospitals. Sometimes people get injured in remote areas, and so an EMT might work in a helicopter, accompanying the victim on a flight to the hospital.

Some EMTs are in the military, working under very difficult circumstances. They might have to run into

Soldiers carry a mock wounded soldier from a medical evacuation helicopter.

a battle to rescue an injured soldier.

Other EMTs work the phone when someone calls 911. These EMTs, called dispatchers, make quick decisions about the type of emergency, and who best to send. Sometimes police officers and firefighters get trained as EMTs.

No matter where they serve, EMTs always stand ready to help those who are sick or injured.

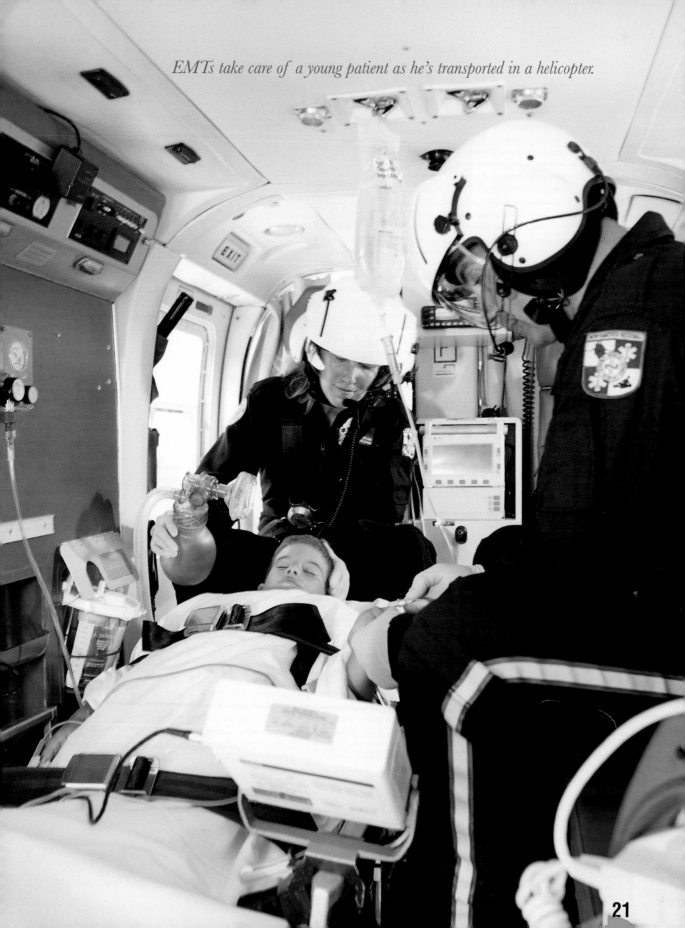

EMTs take care of a young patient as he's transported in a helicopter.

COMMON EMERGENCIES

Car crashes are a common emergency situation for an EMT. In a car crash, there is likely to be a variety of injuries. EMTs must work closely with police officers and firefighters to make sure no more injuries happen. Bumps, bruises, and bleeding are common. If a driver or passenger wasn't wearing a seat belt, the injuries will be much worse. Sometimes, cars are so twisted that emergency personnel need to remove car doors or cut metal out of the way in order to get people out of their cars. EMTs may have to wait until firefighters cut the car open to get the injured person out. It's common to have to immobilize people who have neck and back injuries.

Distracted drivers can cause more crashes.

Another dangerous thing about car accidents is that people who are driving past the accident scene can get distracted. They might be trying to see what is happening. These "rubberneckers" might crash, causing even more injuries. Police try to direct people around the accident scene so no new crashes occur.

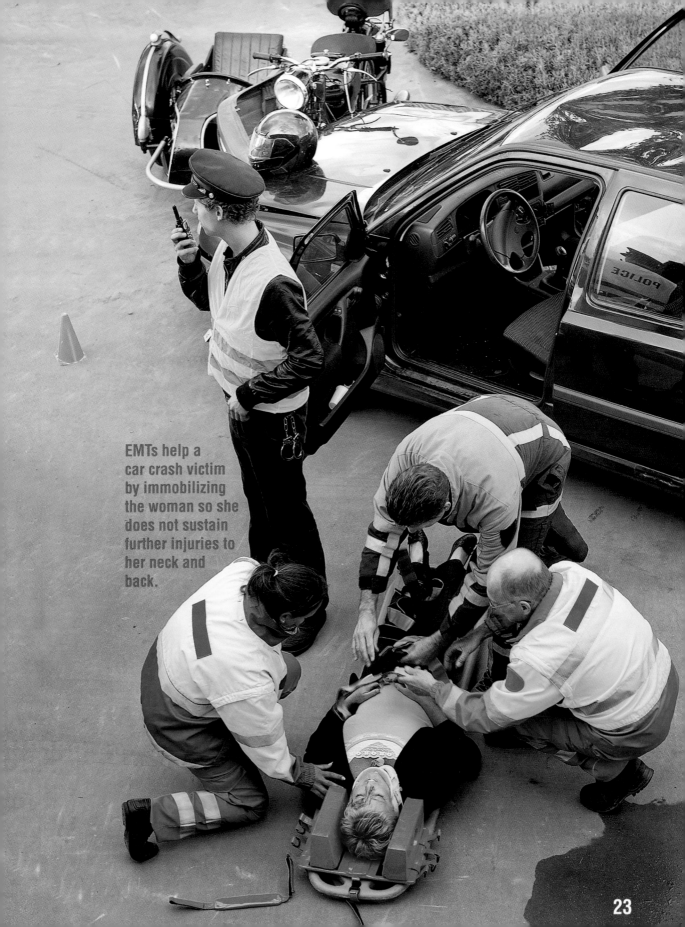

EMTs help a car crash victim by immobilizing the woman so she does not sustain further injuries to her neck and back.

23

An EMT might also be called to a fire. In a fire, there are many things that can injure a person. A person might get burned, or fall through a floor, or hurt themselves as they jump from a window. The most common problem is called *smoke inhalation*. This means that a person has breathed in too much smoke. The number-one cause of death in fires isn't burns, it's breathing in too much smoke. Smoke inhalation is dangerous because the victim doesn't get enough oxygen. The EMT has to give the victim a breathing mask with extra oxygen, and then determine if the person needs more medical treatment.

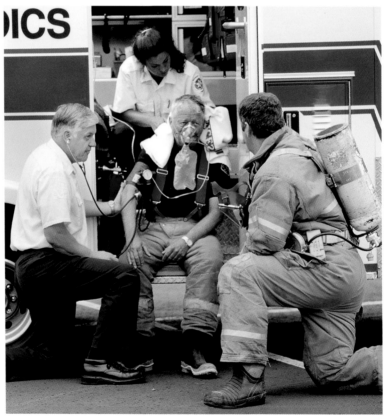

A firefighter is treated for smoke inhalation.

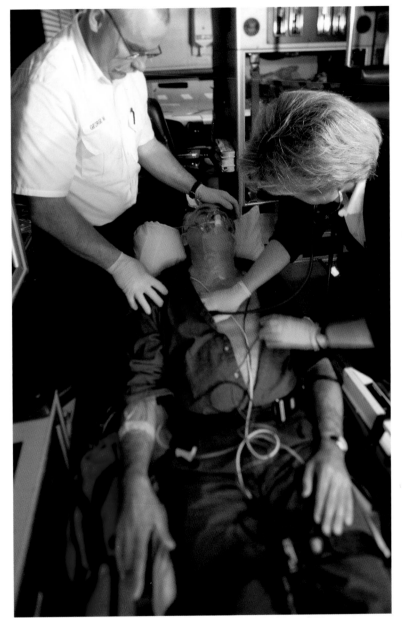

EMTs help a man with chest pains. Paramedics are trained to handle a person having a heart attack. It is a common situation for EMTs.

Another emergency situation where EMTs can be called to help is a heart attack. EMTs often arrive and find a person having severe chest pains. Doctors call it a myocardial infarction, but most people call it a heart attack. It usually happens when a blood clot blocks the flow of blood to the heart. The heart quickly becomes starved for oxygen. Depending on the patient and the EMT's training, the EMT might give the victim oxygen, administer medication, or use an automated external defibrillator to shock the heart back into a normal rhythm.

INTERVIEW WITH AN EMT

Kerry worked and taught as an EMT and EMTP (Emergency Medical Technician-Paramedic) for 10 years. She went back to school to teach college courses, and now works at a university.

Q: How did you get interested in being an EMT?

Kerry: I wanted to learn CPR and basic first aid, so to combine the two I took an EMT course. While I was in the training program, our instructor encouraged us to consider volunteering for a rural ambulance service, and that is how I started as an EMT.

Rural EMTs are often volunteers. Their skills keep people alive until the victims can get to a hospital.

Q: What's an average day like as an EMT?

Kerry: EMTs do shift work, 24 hours a day, like a hospital. They report to base and check in with dispatch. They check out the ambulance to ensure it is fully stocked, clean, and fueled. They wait for calls, or cover other areas when another ambulance goes on a call. There are times when calls are slow, so administrative or educational tasks may be assigned.

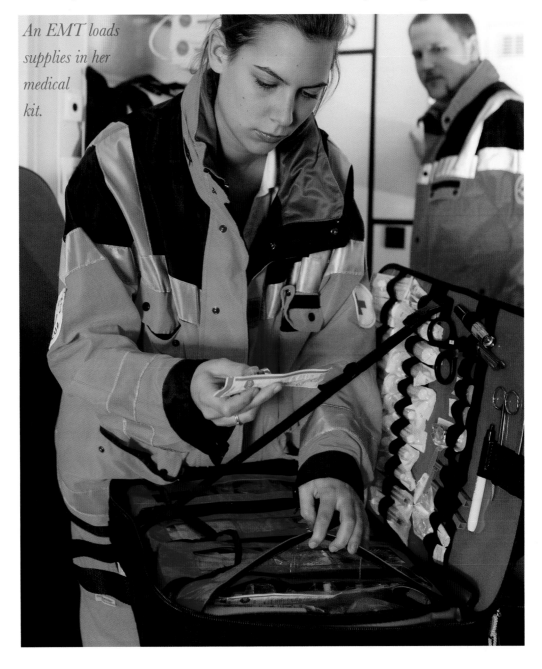

An EMT loads supplies in her medical kit.

Q: What's your most memorable experience as an EMT?

Kerry: Delivering a healthy baby in a family's living room was a great experience. Everyone was very excited. We were in the kitchen of the family's home and the other kids were able to watch as their sister was born.

Q: What's the best part about being an EMT?

Kerry: Helping people is great, and the variety of work situations is interesting. EMTs work with fire departments and police departments, as well as hospital emergency rooms.

EMTs hold a baby born in their ambulance in a parking lot.

Q: What advice would you have for someone who wants to be an EMT?

Kerry: Spend some time talking to and observing people who do this job so you have a realistic picture of what the work is like. It is not like on TV. You need to be flexible and confident because situations change all the time. EMTs work in all kinds of weather and sometimes in unknown situations. Continuing education is also an important part of being an EMT.

EMTs work in all kinds of weather. They face challenging situations every day.

GLOSSARY

ALLERGIC REACTION
The body's extreme response to a foreign substance entering it. An allergic reaction may come from a specific food (such as nuts), pollen (from flowers or trees), or chemicals (such as a bee's venom). A person may have minor to major swelling, difficulty breathing and swallowing, or even a rapid drop in blood pressure and fainting.

ANATOMY
The study of the human body and its internal workings.

BACKBOARD
A hard board placed underneath and secured with straps to a person who has hurt their back or neck. This keeps a patient from moving and further injury.

CPR
Cardiopulmonary resuscitation (CPR) is an emergency procedure in which chest compressions and mouth-to-mouth breathing are conducted on a victim whose heart and lungs have stopped working.

DEFIBRILLATOR
An electrical device used to apply a brief shock to a victim and restore a normal heartbeat.

EMERGENCY MEDICAL SERVICES (EMS)

An organized group of services, including 911 emergency call centers and trained EMTs and paramedics, that helps people in emergency situations get to a hospital for care.

FIRST RESPONDERS

People, such as police, firefighters, EMTs, and paramedics, who are the first on the scene of an emergency situation.

IMMOBILIZE

To secure something so that it can't move. If a person has a neck injury, an EMT will immobilize the head and neck so that the person can be transported safely to a hospital.

MYOCARDIAL INFARCTION

Usually called a heart attack. The most common cause is a blood clot that blocks a blood vessel near the heart, starving the heart of oxygen.

SMOKE INHALATION

Breathing in smoke. Most deaths in fires are due to smoke inhalation.

STROKE

When blood flow to a certain part of the brain is stopped. This results in the sudden death of brain cells and causes such symptoms as paralysis, speech impairment, loss of memory, coma, and even death.

TRIAGE

Making decisions about who is hurt the worst and needs medical attention immediately, and who is hurt but does not need immediate medical help.

INDEX

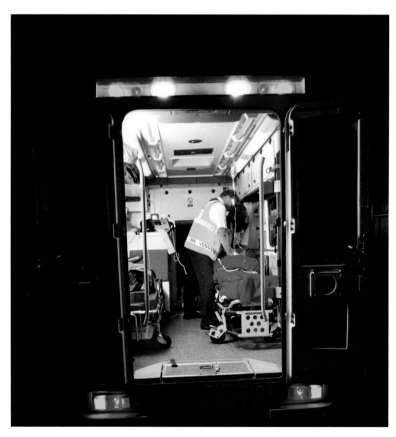